Nothing lives long
Only the earth
And the mountains.

Cheyenne Song

COPYRIGHT © 1990 The Rourke Corporation, Inc.
Vero Beach, Florida 32964
Text © 1990 Terri Cowman
Illustration © 1990 Charles Reasoner

LIBRARY OF CONGRESS CATALOGING-IN-PUBLICATION DATA
Cohlene, Terri, 1950
  Quillworker / by Terri Cohlene; illustrated by Charles Reasoner.
     p. cm. — (Native American legends)

  Summary: A Cheyenne legend explaining the origins of the stars. Also describes the history and
culture of the Cheyenne Indians.
   ISBN 086593 004 X
   1. Cheyenne Indians — Legends. 2. Cheyenne Indians — Social life and customs — Juvenile literature.
(1. Cheyenne Indians — Legends. 2. Cheyenne Indians — Social life and customs. 3. Indians of North
America — Legends. 4. Indians of North America — Social life and customs.) I. Reasoner, Charles, ill.
II. Title. III. Series.
E99.C53C68 1990
398.2 089973 — dc20   AC   CIP   89-10742

NATIVE AMERICAN LEGENDS

Quillworker
A CHEYENNE LEGEND

WRITTEN AND ADAPTED BY TERRI COHLENE

ILLUSTRATED BY CHARLES REASONER

DESIGNED BY VIC WARREN

Watermill Press
Mahwah, N.J.

ong ago, when the moon was alone in the night sky, there lived a Cheyenne girl named Quillworker. She had no brothers or sisters, but her parents were proud of their only child. Her skills with a needle brought praise from tribes all around. The old women in the village were amazed that a girl so young had already decorated thirty buffalo robes, a task that usually took an entire lifetime.

Quillworker would go to the Lodge of the Quillers' Society to teach the younger girls. She would describe how she gathered and dyed the porcupine quills with vibrant colors, then created her beautiful designs. All the while, her fingers would fly as she embroidered yet another pouch or quiver. The old women would argue who among them had taught Quillworker the most, for she was truly gifted.

ne day, as Quillworker sat in her parents' lodge, she cut a war shirt from a soft piece of buckskin. It had buffalo hair fringe on the sleeves and across the front. She worked many weeks, sewing red, blue, yellow, and white quills onto it. The design was magnificent, with each color of quills radiating from another. When she finished her design, she cut a breechclout and leggings from the soft leather, then moccasins and a pair of gauntlets.

Quillworker's mother watched with curiosity. "Daughter, why do you make such a warrior's outfit? Your father has one already and you have no brothers. Neither has your time come for a husband."

"It is true, Mother. I do not know why I must do this, but it came to me in a dream."

"And what is this design? I do not know it."

Quillworker touched the front of the war shirt. "It is beautiful, is it not? It too came to me in my sleep."

Her mother nodded. "You are wise to heed your dreams, Daughter. That is how the spirits guide us."

For many suns and moons, Quillworker labored. When she finished the garment, she tied all the pieces together in a parfleche decorated to match. She then tanned more buckskin and made another war shirt like the one she'd just completed.

This she did six more times, and each time her mother asked, "Daughter, why do you make this warrior's garment?"

And each time, Quillworker answered, "I do not know, Mother. It came to me in a dream." As she completed the seventh garment, Quillworker wondered at its size. It was smaller than the others, as if it were for a boy instead of a man. To this last bundle, she also added a quiver, decorated with the same radiant design.

6

Quillworker's task was finished. She bundled clothing for herself around her quilling needles and filled her parfleche with food stores she'd been putting aside. She took dried turnips, thistle stalks, milkweed buds, chokecherry pemmican, and dried deer meat. She also packed her knife, tanning kit, and cooking utensils.

When Quillworker's mother saw her preparing for a journey, she asked, "Daughter, where are you going?"

Quillworker smiled. "Seven days from here is the tipi of seven brothers. These clothes are for them. I am to be their sister, and one day, they will be admired by all The People."

"Then that is as it should be, Daughter. I will help you ready your things."

They busied themselves attaching a travois to each of two dogs. Quillworker was ready to leave.

"How do you know the way?" asked her mother.

"I don't know how," she answered, "but it came to me in my dreams. I will not become lost."

Quillworker bade her mother goodbye, and with the dogs following her, she walked in the direction of the mountains.

Six days she walked, eating meals of pemmican and fresh berries and sipping from her water pouch. At night, she wrapped herself in buffalo robes and slept by a small fire. Her dreams were her guide for the following day's journey.

Finally, on the seventh day, she came upon a stream. On the other side, near a grove of trees, stood a large tipi. Could this be the lodge of the seven brothers? It was covered by more than twenty buffalo hides. From the top of the lifting pole flew a long braid of buffalo hair.

As she and the dogs approached the water, a boy stepped from inside the tipi. "It is I," Quillworker called out, "Seeker-of-Seven-Brothers. I bring gifts."

The boy raised his hand in greetings. "I am Wihio, the youngest of seven brothers. And you are Quillworker, our new sister. I was expecting you."

"You were? Did you see me in a dream?"

Wihio shook his head. "I sent you the dream. I have the Power of Knowing and the Power of Sky-Reaching."

"What is 'Sky-Reaching'?" asked the sister.

"You will see," answered Wihio. "The brothers are hunting, but they will return soon. Come, I'll show you our lodge."

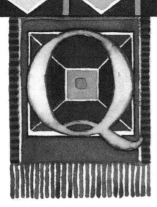

uillworker untied the parfleches from the travois and sent the dogs back to her mother. She stepped inside the tipi and saw seven buffalo robes covering seven beds of woven mats. She gave Wihio his buckskin garment and laid the others out on the beds. How beautiful they were. How they shone. Wihio quickly tried on his new clothes while his sister went outside to gather grasses for her bed.

"This is the buckskin of a mighty warrior," said Wihio when Quillworker returned. He put his arrows in the new quiver. "The brothers will be happy too. I did not tell them you were coming. What a wonderful surprise this will be."

Singing her Song of Home, Quillworker gathered wood for the fire and started a pot of stew. She cooked turnips and milkweed buds. There will be buffalo meat when the hunters return, she thought.

She was right. Soon the six brothers arrived. Wihio met them outside the tipi. "What is that you're wearing?" the eldest asked. "And what is that delicious smell?"

Wihio did a small dance to show off his war costume. "Quillworker, our new sister, brought this for me. She brought garments for you too. Come inside and meet her. She's preparing a meal for us now."

The seven brothers were happy to have a sister. They admired the new war shirts, which fit perfectly.

"What handsome brothers you are," Quillworker said shyly.

"What a beautiful and talented sister you are," the brothers answered. "Wihio surprises us with his gift of Knowing, but we are pleased."

And so it was for several moons. Every day, the elder brothers left to hunt while Wihio practiced with his arrows near the lodge. Quillworker spent mornings gathering fuel and digging roots or picking berries. She prepared buffalo meat to dry in the sun and tanned hides for clothing.

One morning, Quillworker and Wihio were alone in the lodge. Suddenly they heard hoofbeats and scratching at the tipi door. In his bravest voice, the little brother asked, "Who is it, and what do you want?"

"I am Buffalo Calf," was the answer. "I was sent by the buffalo nation for your sister."

Wihio put his head out the door and saw the calf standing there. "Why do you want our sister?"

"She is beautiful and makes buffalo hides beautiful. We want to be beautiful too."

Quillworker was afraid. She did not want to go with the calf.

Wihio closed the flap. "Go away. You can't have her."

"If you won't give me your sister, someone bigger than I will come."

"No. Go away." said Wihio. And the calf left.

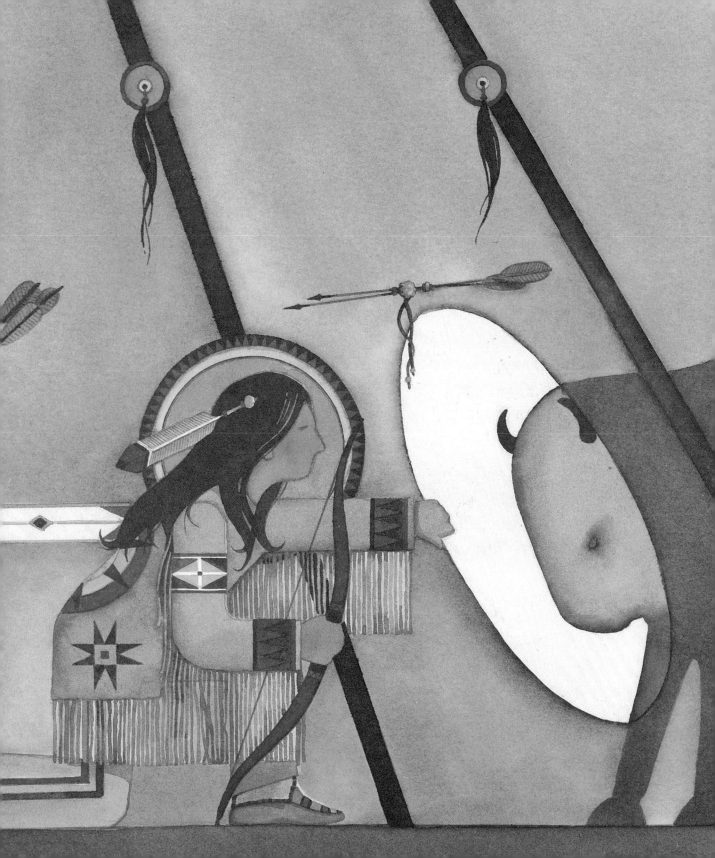

The next morning, they again heard hoofbeats
and scratching on the tipi.

"Who is it?" demanded Wihio.

"It is I, Buffalo Cow. I've come for your sister."

Wihio put his head out the door. "Go away,"
he said to the cow. "You can't have her."

The buffalo snorted. "You don't know what
you're saying. If you don't give her to me, someone
greater than I will come, and he won't be alone.
They will kill you."

Quillworker's heart beat fast. Would her
brother make her go?

Wihio closed the flap. "I don't care. You
can't have her. Go away." And the cow left.

he next morning, the older brothers stayed home to protect their sister. They were all sitting around the fire when they felt the earth tremble. They heard thundering hoofbeats that seemed to come from every direction, followed by stamping and snorting and bellowing. Then there were loud scraping sounds on the tipi. It seemed as if the hides would tear.

All seven brothers looked out the entrance hole. As the clouds of dust settled, they saw the gigantic bull buffalo. He was bigger than any they'd ever seen before, and the entire buffalo nation was pawing the ground behind him. "Give us your sister or we'll kill you all," roared the bull.

Quillworker was afraid. The brothers were afraid. Then Wihio stepped out of the lodge. "I am not afraid of you."

The bull looked down on the boy. "Then you are a fool, for you will surely die. If you won't give us your sister, we'll take her from you." The giant buffalo glared with blood red eyes as he blew his hot breath on Wihio.

The six older brothers brought Quillworker
out of the tipi. Wihio drew an arrow from his
new quiver. "Jump into that tree!" he yelled.
"I will use my Power of Sky-Reaching!"
As his sister and six brothers caught branches
of the nearby tree, Wihio shot his arrow into its
trunk. Then he caught the lowest branch,
and the tree grew a thousand feet upward.

uillworker and her brothers looked down at the startled herd. Even from this distance, they could see the bull's anger. "This will do you no good," he roared, and charged the tree with his horns.

Wood splintered and the tree shook. "He will break the tree!" shouted Quillworker.

Wihio sat astride his branch and drew a second arrow, sending it deep into the trunk. The tree instantly grew to the height of a mountain. Below, the herd appeared very small, but the sister and brothers could still hear the animals bellowing.

"Give us your sister!" roared the bull. Then he crashed into the trunk once again. The tree shook so hard, everyone nearly fell out.

Wihio removed his last arrow from the quiver and set it to his bow. He released it high into the branches and at once, the tree pushed through the clouds. "Quickly!" he ordered. "Step onto the cloud. Do not be afraid."

No sooner had they done this than the buffalo charged again, this time sending the tree crashing to the ground. Quillworker looked down. "We are safe from the buffalo, little brother, but we have come too far. How can we return?"

Wihio stretched his arms to the heavens. "This is our home now.
We shall become stars."

As he said this, the starburst designs on their buckskins glowed brighter and brighter, enveloping the sister and seven brothers with brilliant light.

On clear nights, you can see them still. Wihio is the North Star, who swings the others around him like a giant water dipper. The brightest star is Quillworker, whose fingers never rest. To this day, she embroiders the night sky with her shimmering designs.

THE CHEYENNE

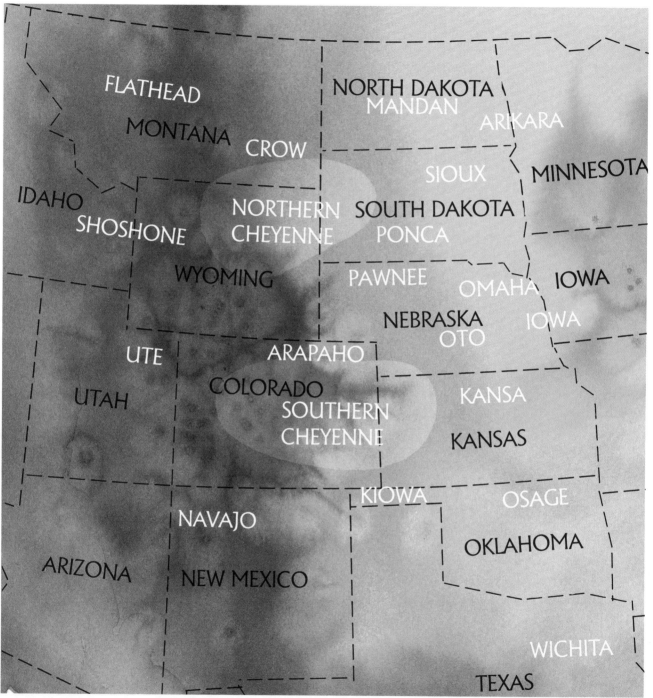

The Cheyenne lived in two different parts of the Plains.

CHEYENNE HOMELAND

Long ago, the Cheyenne people lived in earth lodges near Lake Superior. It was a fertile woodland where they raised corn, beans, and squash. The men did not often need to hunt.

After Spanish explorers introduced horses, the Cheyenne gave up their permanent village homes to follow the buffalo herds on the Great Plains.

Buffalo were all-important to the plains way of life. They provided food, utensils, clothing, and shelter. At one time there were herds of up to a hundred million buffalo.

The Plains life was not always easy. In the summer, prairie winds blew and it could be hotter than 100 degrees. In the winter, it could drop to 40 degrees below zero with heavy snows. Even so, the land was dry, and when it rained, it often flooded.

The Cheyenne were handsome people like this young family. They were sometimes called "the Beautiful People".

CHEYENNE PEOPLE

They called themselves "Tsistsista," meaning "The People." The Sioux called them "Sahiyena," or "foreign talker." The white settlers had trouble pronouncing this name, so instead called them "Cheyenne."

Women tanned hides, made tipis and furnishings, wove mats and sewed and decorated clothing. They gathered and prepared food, collected fuel, cared for the children, and moved the camp. The men hunted, tended the horses, made weapons, waged war, and performed important religious ceremonies. The elders instructed the young by teaching proper behavior and tribal history.

Once millions of buffalo roamed the plains, and the Cheyenne people followed the herds.

Dogs as well as horses moved the tribe's belongings across the plains on platforms called travois.

Two Moons was a great Cheyenne chief. His headdress is made of buffalo horns and ermine skins.

THE CHEYENNE CAMP

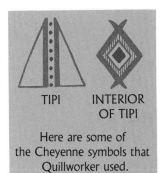

TIPI   INTERIOR
        OF TIPI

Here are some of
the Cheyenne symbols that
Quillworker used.

The People lived in tipi villages. One of the tipi's most important features was that it could be moved easily. The framework was made of long, sturdy poles and was covered with buffalo skins. When a family needed a new tipi, the wife spent many weeks tanning hides. Then she and her friends could construct a new tipi in a day.

Making the outside was only half the job. Inside, there were simple furnishings. Beds made of grass or buffalo hair padding were covered by buffalo robes. Back rests for each bed were made of sticks and reeds. Belongings were kept underneath.

The inside wall was covered with a dew cloth, preventing rain from dripping inside. In the center of the lodge burned the fire, used for light, heat, and cooking.

Cheyenne families lived in villages of tipis much like this Blackfoot camp.

Women in this village are stretching buffalo hides. Buffalo meat hangs to dry in the sun.

CLOTHING

Women tanned animal hides for clothing. This is the process of making animal skin into leather. Hides were soaked in water overnight then scraped and cleaned. Next, a chemical mixture of buffalo brains, liver, and soapweed was applied. Then the hides were shaved and softened by pulling them back and forth through a hole in a buffalo shoulder bone.

Women and girls wore short-sleeved dresses reaching below their knees. At their belts, they wore a hair-covered bag containing their needles and thread. Moccasins made of soft leather uppers and hard rawhide soles protected their feet. In cold weather, they wore leggings and buffalo robes.

Men and boys wore shirts similar to the women's dresses, but shorter and with longer sleeves. A breechclout hung from a belt around the waist.

The Cheyennes decorated their clothing and leather goods with quillwork. Many designs had special meanings and could be recognized by all their people. It was an honor to belong to the Quillers' Society.

The first step to quillworking is the difficult removal of the sharp quills from the porcupines. They are then dyed, using berries, flowers or minerals. After sun-drying the quills, the quillworker flattens them with her teeth so they can be sewn with a bone needle and sinew thread.

This painting shows Cheyenne warriors on horseback in battle with another tribe. Their headdresses were made with eagle feathers.

A young Sioux woman in a deerskin dress embroidered with porcupine quills and beads.

IMPORTANT DATES

1492 Columbus discovers the New World

1760 Spanish introduce horses to the Great Plains

1776 United States declares independence from Britain

1803 Louisiana Purchase

1812-14 War of 1812 between U.S. and Britain

1861-64 Cheyenne-Arapaho War, Native Americans lose Battle of Sand Creek

1861-65 U.S. Civil War

1867-83 Extermination of over 13 million buffalo by white traders

1876 Cheyenne, Sioux & Arapaho win Battle of Little Big Horn

42

This beautiful Teton Dakota quillwork bag is much like the pieces made by the Cheyenne.

After the porcupine quills were dyed different colors, the quills were wrapped around strips of buffalo hide, and the strips were sewn onto hides or clothing.

1924	All Native Americans born in U.S. declared citizens
1890	Battle of Wounded Knee ends the Indian wars
1892	Cheyenne-Arapaho Reservation established
1968	Indian Civil Rights Act giving Native Americans the right to govern themselves on their reservations

The Cheyennes' most famous ceremony was the Sun Dance. It was painful but very important.
These two young Cheyenne men have put on special ceremonial paint for the dance.

GLOSSARY

Breechclout: Worn by men and boys, this soft square of leather hangs from the waist by a belt.

Gauntlets: These were worn at the wrist to protect the hunter from being snapped by the bowstring.

Leggings: A garment similar to pantlegs, tied to the belt.

Lifting Pole: The last pole of the tipi. The skins are attached to it and lifted into place to complete the lodge.

Parfleche: A leather bag, often decorated, used for storage.

Pemmican: A cross between fruit leather and beef jerky, made by mixing dried chokecherries, animal fat, and dried meat.

Sinew: Tendon found along the backbone of the buffalo, used for sewing thread.

Travois: A carrier pulled by a horse, dog, or person. Two poles are crossed and tied at one end, a leather pad is attached to the other.

Wihio: Cheyenne word for 'spider.' Literally, 'one who spins a web and moves up and down, seemingly walking on nothing.' Wihio also means one with higher intelligence.

Hunting buffalo on horseback was dangerous work, and Cheyenne hunters had to be excellent riders.

PHOTO CREDITS

Page 33: Three Fingers, Southern Cheyenne Chief, 1870s. Kansas State Historical Society, E99 C53.I TF *2.

Page 35: Cheyenne Family—Chief Powder Face, Wife and Child, near Hays, Kansas, 1869. Kansas State Historical Society, E99 C53.I PF *1.

Page 36: As It Was In The Old Days, Buffalo Herd, South Dakota, photo by Edward S. Curtis. Special Collections Division, University of Washington Libraries, UW 10912.

Page 37 A Blackfoot Travois, photo by Edward S. Curtis. Special Collections Division, University of Washington Libraries, UW 10910.

Page 38: Two Moons—Cheyenne, 1910, photo by Edward S. Curtis. Special Collections Division, University of Washington Libraries, UW 10911.

Page 39: Blackfoot Camp, hand-colored photograph by Walter McClintock, 1896-1906. Southwest Museum, CT 313.

Page 40: Cheyenne Women Dressing Buffalo Hides. Stanley J. Morrow Collection, W.H. Over State Museum, University of South Dakota, N180.

Page 41: Detail, painted muslin, Cheyenne?, late 19th century. Southwest Museum, CT 93.

Page 42: Sioux Girl, photo by Edward S. Curtis. Special Collections Division, University of Washington Libraries, UW 10909.

Page 43: Teton Dakota Quillwork Bag, 1890s. Southwest Museum, CT 138.

Page 44: Sun Dance Pledgers—Cheyenne, 1911, photo by Edward S. Curtis. Special Collections Division, University of Washington Libraries, UW 10913.

Page 45: Buffalo Chase, painting by Seth Eastman. In the Capitol, Washington, D.C. (National Graphic Center.)

Page 47: Cheyenne Warriors, photo by Edward S. Curtis; Special Collections Division, University of Washington Libraries, UW 11109.